Finding the Sweetness of Life

Judy Bishop Woods

intellect
Publishing ™

www.IntellectPublishing.com

V-11HB

All photography by Judy Bishop Woods

Author: Judy Bishop Woods
ISBN: 978-1-945190-65-0
Copyright 2019 Judy Bishop Woods

Finding the Sweetness of Life

Within these pages may you find a soothing space
to replenish, restore, and grow.

Pause here awhile and discover the nurturing essence
of your own personal mysteries.

You are never being "punished"
but at times you choose to hide.

Hiding is not a bad thing
so don't judge yourself.

You started this phase of the journey
when you intended to allow gracefully,
whatever came up in your life.

Pay attention to what your body is telling you.

It is asking you to be kind to it.

New birth is frustrating sometimes.
Relax. Be patient.

You are experiencing a softening.

Observe.
        Watch it grow.
All is well.

Hiding can be a good way to incubate
while holding space for the new.
New awareness.
        New understanding.
                New energetic templates.

The softening is a way of allowing
 changes to take hold,
to get comfortably seated within you
with grace and ease.

This is an organic transformation
whose time has come.
Old triggers will cease to work.
Instead, love will guide you.

You will find yourself tuning in
to feelings, concepts, people,
that support your evolving in the Light.

You have created it
        And it is so.

Each day brings with it more opportunities.
Pay attention to the ones that
feel right for you.

Pause often, and allow yourself to let go.
Find that place of trust, and intend peace.

Be the peace.

Peace is an active, vibrant state
triggered by your intention.

Practice often this state of being.

You are the physical Light of God.

Turn on this Light
        and remember,
                all is well.

When it is hard for you to be ok
with your current physical expression,
understand that this is where you are
learning to be kind to yourself.

Allowing your current physical expression
        to flow through you
                with grace and ease
                        is the learning.

Trust that the discomfort is the perfect expression
to bring you to a new point of awareness.

Let it all flow
and be the observer of the journey.

Stay focused and be in the grace
of your high heart.

All is well.

Trust the timing of the unfolding in your life.

When is the perfect time for a baby bird
to take its first flight?

You are supported, just as it is.
Feel this supportive life force energy
        flowing through you.

You cannot force it.
It simply is.
This flowing force carries you forward
        in perfect timing.

There is nowhere to rush to.
All is simply an unfolding of your life's journey.

Embrace the rhythm of it
        as it ebbs and flows.

All is well.

For you, the energetic template will feel like
the peace of all ages throughout time and beyond.

You simply will not be drawn in
by the lower vibrational energies.

As you experience life,
you will be drawn
to the exquisite sweetness of it.

Your higher energy bodies are being enlivened
to vibrate more fully in this dance.

And what is not in attunement
will fall away.

Watch.
It is already happening.

All is well.

Sometimes you feel like you are being
swept backwards,
still in the grip of old patterns.

Yet at the same time you are moving forward
into new energetic patterns.
Do not try to make this happen.
Just be observant.

Watch for the new,
        and relax into it.
                Let it unfold.

You have sown the seeds and they are sprouting.
The young, tender shoots of new consciousness
        will fascinate you.

And the old, tired thought forms will fall away
        through lack of attention.

The new beckons to you,
        and is ripe with inspiration
                in which you will experience true joy.

In the stillness comes the recalibration.
Sometimes it only takes a moment,
sometimes longer.

Trust the rhythm of this timing.
The quiet times are life-supporting,
giving you new nourishment.

Honor them.
    Respect them.

Sometimes it feels like nothing is happening.
But so much is happening.
Allow.
    Allow.
        Allow.
And breathe into the allowing.

Nothing is more important
    than your relationship with you.

Find your inner peace
    and just be.

Joy is not a fleeting thing.

It is more like an underground spring.
Its source is constant
but it does not always rise
to the surface.

Trust that it is there
        deep within you.

Sometimes it splashes forth,
        life-giving.
And when it does
it bathes you
in its effervescent flow.

Joy is always within you,
        and its source is love.

Let it out.
        Let it flow.
                All is well.

As you move into your day,
do so with an attitude of gratefulness.

All that you experience in each new day,
adds to your growing awareness.

Be aware of what you are desiring.
Your desires bring you the gifts of learning.

Try desiring ways to express joy,
and then watch what happens.

Breathe.
Breathe in and receive
    all the blessings
        that life is offering to you.

Breathe out, giving thanks
    for those blessings.

When we open to receive,
we signal the Universe
that we are ready for Its gifts.

By giving gratitude,
we become an active participant
in the process.

The life force moving through us
is never static
but it can be magnified
by our attention to it.

Relax.
    Breathe.
        All is well.

As you seek,
Much is revealed,
But you are still the decider.

What feels good to you now?

What can you relax into?

Searching is grand.
It moves you forward.
It helps you to realize,
        to understand,
                who you truly are.

What is calling to you now?

Is it bringing you joy?
        A smile?
                Laughter?

Let your search bring these to you
and allow the expansiveness to continue.

A new day dawns
    replete with gifts.

Which ones will you choose to receive?

Fill yourself to overflowing
    and you will naturally become the giver.

This is the way of happiness.

Open up to the harmony of life.

There is a natural rhythm happening constantly.

As you tune into it
you will find that
it is all around you…

The rustling of the leaves,
    lapping of the waves,
        calling of the birds.

Nature is always dancing to this harmonious flow.

And you are being invited to join in.

Open up.
    Feel the rhythm.
        Let it flow.

Thoughts...

Thoughts…

About the Author

*I received these insights through mediations at a time
when I was asking for clarity and encouragement.*

*A source of comfort and inspiration for me,
it is my hope that they will be for you also.*

**Judy Bishop Woods is an artist, a photographer, and a writer
residing in Fairhope, Alabama.**

*If you wish to buy additional books or communicate with
the author you may reach her through the website:*

www.FindingThe SweetnessOfLife.com